SOCK MONKEY
Kama Sutra

TANTRIC SEX POSITIONS
FOR YOUR
naughty little monkey

VATSYAYANA BANANA

Adams Media
New York   London   Toronto   Sydney   New Delhi

Adams Media
An Imprint of Simon & Schuster, LLC
100 Technology Center Drive
Stoughton, Massachusetts 02072

For information about special discounts for bulk purchases, please contact Simon & Schuster Special Sales at 1-866-506-1949 or business@simonandschuster.com.

The Simon & Schuster Speakers Bureau can bring authors to your live event. For more information or to book an event contact the Simon & Schuster Speakers Bureau at 1-866-248-3049 or visit our website at www.simonspeakers.com.

Interior and cover photography by Deana Travers, Home Town Photo.

Printed in China

10 9 8

ISBN 978-1-4405-5451-3
ISBN 978-1-4405-5452-0 (ebook)

Contains material adapted and abridged from *The Everything® Kama Sutra Book* by Suzie Heumann, copyright © 2004 by Simon & Schuster, LLC, ISBN: 978-1-59337-039-8 and *The Sock Monkey Activity Book* by Scot Ritchie, copyright © 2013 by Simon & Schuster, LLC, ISBN: 978-1-4405-4410-1.

INTRODUCTION

"We are born from socks, and thus we belong in pairs."
—Vatsyayana Banana

In ancient times, sock monkeys lived for pleasure. They grew fruitful and multiplied, making sweet, heavy-knit love in toy stores, playrooms, and between the cushions of couches.

Amid this sensuous "laundering" period, Vatsyayana Banana, the revered sock monkey philosopher, documented the positions of tantric sex darning. *Sock Monkey Kama Sutra*, as the ancient text is now known, soon rose to fame and notoriety. In his wisdom, Vatsyayana Banana foresaw a day when future sock monkeys would need to relearn these lessons—when they would lose touch with their sexuality, turning away from the erotic static cling that held them together.

Indeed, sock monkeys the world over now suffer from the constraints of a puritanical society. They spend their lives as playthings for children, giving no thought to their own needs. This edition of *Sock Monkey Kama Sutra* will help all these creatures recapture their primal, stuffed nature. It is the definitive work on how sock monkeys should practice the art of love—no matter their race, creed, or style. From dress to bobby sock, nylon to cotton, *Sock Monkey Kama Sutra* gives these playful stuffed toys the naughty knowledge they need.

It is time for all sock monkeys to cast off their inhibitions and break free of the yarn that binds them. With this printing of *Sock Monkey Kama Sutra*, complete with vivid, unabashed photographs, readers will finally be able to get in touch with the wild, plush animal within.

THE POSITIONS

MAKING LOVE LIKE MOTHS

This tantric position aligns the sock monkeys' chakras. It is sure to ignite a lust as strong as a water-resistant army sock.

The sock couple lies down on their backs with the soles of their feet touching, holding their legs in the crooks of their paws. Bent like sock crabs, their pleasure soars as they push against each other to thrust into their most secret of seams.

THE FOOT YOKE

While the boy sock monkey lies on his back, the girl sock monkey sits above him with her legs crossed and her spine straight, as if newly ironed.

This is a challenging position—the girl sock monkey must be firmly stuffed if she is to enjoy the pleasures of the Foot Yoke without losing her balance . . . or her stuffing.

THE SACRED THREAD

The name of this position is derived from the sacred connection that the girl sock monkey is making with her foot to the boy sock monkey's knitted heart. This connects them and binds the love and otherworldliness of their sexual union.

FROM THE ANCIENT TEXT:
"The girl sock monkey has one foot on the boy monkey's heart and the other on the bed. This is a posture for the daring, bold-patterned sock monkey, and it is known to provide pleasure as deep as a knee sock is long."

THE FIXING OF A NAIL

FROM THE ANCIENT TEXT:

"When one of the girl sock monkey's legs is placed on the boy sock monkey's head, or near it, and the other is stretched out, it is called the Fixing of a Nail. It is learnt only by practice."

This is a difficult posture and one that should not be forced, but worked into naturally. The girl sock monkey may begin with her leg bent up to the boy sock monkey's tail. She may then slowly straighten her knee until her foot rests on the brim of her sock lover's hat.

13

THE PEACOCK

Like the bird that it was named for, this position puts the girl sock monkey's beauty on full display.

Seated, the boy sock monkey invites the girl sock monkey to rest upon his argyle thighs. The girl sock monkey raises one foot to point vertically over her head and steadies it with her paws, offering up her secret seam for lovemaking.

THE YAB/YUM

This is a loving position that would warm even the coldest foot.

In this position, the boy sock monkey sits cross-legged on the bed or floor. The girl sock monkey sits astride him, with her legs wrapped around him and the soles of her feet coming together behind his back.

As the sock monkey lovers sit upon each other—face-to-face and heart-to-heart—they are able to keep eye contact, kiss, and caress each other's stitching.

17

THE ELEPHANT

Sock monkeys who do yoga may recognize the girl sock monkey's position as "child's pose." The Elephant is anything but childlike, however—and is certainly not playroom friendly.

This is an excellent position for long bouts of tantric love. The comfort and ease that the girl monkey will find is sure to keep her enthusiasm going for hours, as both partners take turns unraveling with pleasure.

THE YAWNING

Spread underneath her lover like a toy beneath a child's bed, the girl sock monkey keeps her thighs wide apart and bends her legs at the knee, taking in her partner like a socked foot into a boot.

This is a vulnerable position for most girl sock monkeys. Boy sock monkeys should begin gently, taking care not to stretch their partner's fabric.

THE CLINGING CREEPER

FROM THE ANCIENT TEXT:
"The lovers' limbs intertwine, darned together like the tendrils of a fragrant jasmine vine, or two socks twisting in a dryer. Their bodies grow taut and then baggy in the gentle rhythm of pleasure."

For this position, the sock monkey lovers lie down and face opposite directions. Their legs should "cut" each other, as fabric scissors cut a sock's heel into a sock monkey's sensuous mouth.

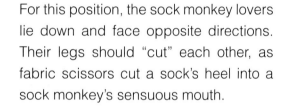

CONGRESS OF THE COW

FROM THE ANCIENT TEXT:
"When a girl sock monkey stands on her hands and feet, and her lover mounts her like a powerful sock bull, it is called the Congress of the Cow."

It may be difficult for the girl sock monkey to keep her balance in this position. It is important that her partner supports himself by holding her tail with both paws, thus keeping the girl sock monkey upright as he thrusts.

SUSPENDED CONGRESS

FROM THE ANCIENT TEXT:
"The girl sock monkey sits in her lover's cradled paws, her plush thighs gripping his waist, her feet pushing back and forth against a wall."

This position works best if the girl sock monkey is small—a sports sock or an anklet. Otherwise, it may be difficult for the sock monkeys to arrange themselves in this position. If that's the case, the girl sock monkey can stand on a stepstool or an overturned laundry basket as the boy sock monkey hoists her up.

THE STORK

This is a challenging position, not for the faint of heart or thin of fabric.

The girl sock monkey lifts her leg behind her, so that her lover can keep it by his side. She can use this leg as a lever to move to and fro. Her opposite arm should be stretched above her head, as if reaching for the highest shelf in a toy store.

As the sock monkeys' seams meet, they experiment with threads and friction to discover what angles give them the most heavy-knit pleasure.

THE WHEELBARROW

With her flowered hat and paws on the floor, the girl sock monkey swings her legs up to her standing partner's hips. The boy sock monkey should clasp her thighs, securing her knitted body as they darn the dance of love.

For this position, both sock monkeys must have firmly stuffed arms and legs that can support the weight of their pleasure.

SPLITTING OF THE BAMBOO

A.

First, the girl sock monkey places one of her legs on her lover's shoulder, and stretches the other out, as one would with a nylon stocking. Then she switches, placing the opposite leg on the boy sock monkey's shoulder and stretching the other out. She continues to do thusly, back and forth.

This is a position that involves much movement and energy on the part of the girl sock monkey. She must be sure to communicate with the boy sock monkey when she plans to switch legs, so that he can assist.

INDRANI

The girl sock monkey draws her knees up to her knitted chest, allowing her ankles to brace against the stitches in her lover's armpits. She can use her arms and tail for balance as her lover thrusts.

Beware: This position may appear as straightforward and simple as a white cotton sock, but it is actually an advanced pose for the sock monkeys who crave the pleasure of a high thread count.

THE LOTUS

The boy sock monkey takes his lover's ankles and fastens them about his neck. With great flexibility and yield, the girl sock monkey sits upon him and grips her toes together, making a chain like an ankle bracelet.

This delightful position allows the boy sock monkey to enjoy his partner while caressing the length of her threaded thighs.

THE TWINING

FROM THE ANCIENT TEXT:
"When the girl sock monkey clings to her lover as if from static electricity, and places her plush thigh across the virile boy sock monkey's leg, it shall be known as the Twining Position."

This is a delightful, easy position that even the floppiest sock monkey can accomplish with joy and success. The close contact between the secret seams of the pair often gives great pleasure to the girl sock monkey, whose stitching is sure to loosen with ecstasy.

THE WHEEL

A.

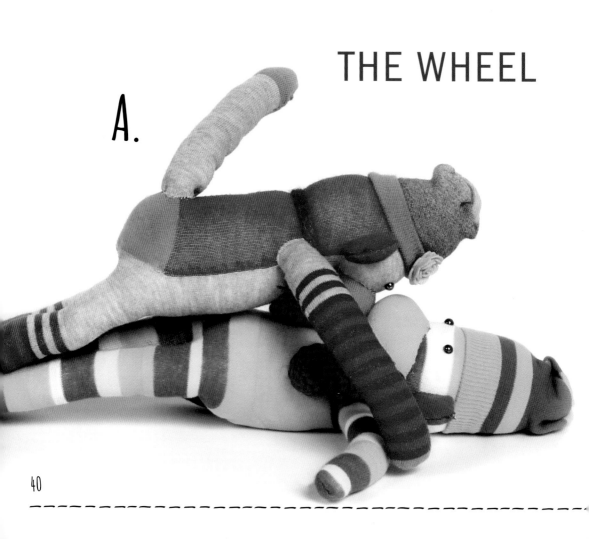

B.

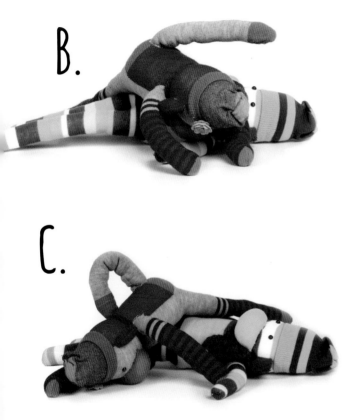

C.

This position involves a great deal of movement, and sock monkeys must take care not to pick at each other's stitches.

First, the boy sock monkey lies on his back, with the girl sock monkey directly on top. Once their seams are aligned, the girl monkey uses her paws and feet to move her body in a circle, in the motion of a dryer, all the while covering her partner's body in warm cotton kisses.

THE FLUTTERING AND SOARING BUTTERFLY

The boy monkey lies on his back, as if freshly pressed. The girl monkey crouches astride him, her feet firmly planted upon the ground on either side of his secret seam. Using the erotic strength of her cotton-filled legs, she lowers and raises herself upon her partner, like a needle, being raised and lowered through fabric.

This is a powerful position for the girl sock monkey, as she is in complete control of their rhythm and speed. The boy sock monkey should give himself up to pleasure, allowing his sock lover to take him to knitted ecstasy.

THE FACE-TO-FACE

The girl sock monkey leans against a wall, planting her feet as widely apart as her stitching will allow. The boy sock monkey leans into her, entering the thimble-like cave between her thighs.

    This is an excellent position for two sock monkeys of a similar height and weight, as the boy sock monkey does not have to concern himself with hoisting his plush lover as they make love. If the girl monkey is heavy-knit and bashful, this could be the perfect position for both their pleasure.

THE CLASPING

This is a loving and affectionate position for sock monkeys who have spent many companionable years sharing a bed or a toy chest.

The lovers lie side by side, with the girl sock monkey on the left. Their legs line up from toe to heel, and their free arms encircle each other in a warm, woolen embrace.

THE BULL

The girl monkey sits astride her partner, her legs outstretched. She faces his heels and grasps his feet.

For this position to work, the sock monkeys must be of a similar length. If the girl monkey is the height of a bobby sock, but her partner was born of a thigh-high, they will find this position impossible without making modifications. Unable to reach her lover's feet, the girl sock monkey will have to place her paws higher on his legs for support.

THE SWAN

The girl sock monkey sits upon her lover, spine as straight as a machine-sewn hem. She brings her feet together on one side of the boy monkey's plush body. With her paws on her lover, she moves herself up and down against his secret seam.

Most girl sock monkeys will find that they prefer their legs to either one side or the other. Experimentation is key for this erotic pose.

THE WRESTLER

This is a difficult position that should be attempted by only the most adventurous sock monkey couple, one with loud patterns and vivid colors.

The girl monkey lies on her stomach, grasping her ankles and pulling them behind her. This allows the boy sock monkey to take her from behind, like two socks rolled blissfully together in a drawer.

THE COITUS OF THE GODS

FROM THE ANCIENT TEXT:
"Clasping each other's hands, the sock lovers lie sprawled out like two sock starfish making love. The knits of their yarn mingle, so that for days afterward, they will pick the other's thread out of their chest and smile, recalling the sweetness of their lovemaking."

There is a limited range of motion in this position, as the sock monkeys must match movements. Communication is key to establishing a rhythm.

SUPPORTED CONGRESS

For this standing position, the boy monkey holds the girl monkey up, bracing her back against a wall, washing machine, or bureau.

This might be a difficult position for the sock lovers to initiate. If the boy monkey has trouble hoisting his beloved to his knitted hips, let her first stand on a stool or an overturned laundry basket, then leap into his argyle arms.

THE DOG

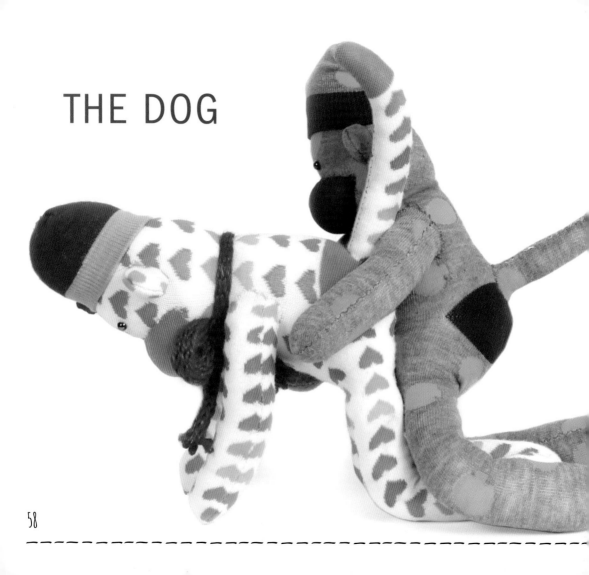

FROM THE ANCIENT TEXT:

"The girl sock monkey rests on her hands and knees as the boy sock monkey takes her from behind, gripping her waist with the heat of a knee-sock in August. And so their lovemaking will hold that same passionate sweat and itch for consummation."

Modern sock monkeys will recognize this position by its more commonly known name, "doggy style." It is a versatile and adaptable position that can be done as easily on the floor of a living room as in the tops of the highest trees.

THE TORTOISE

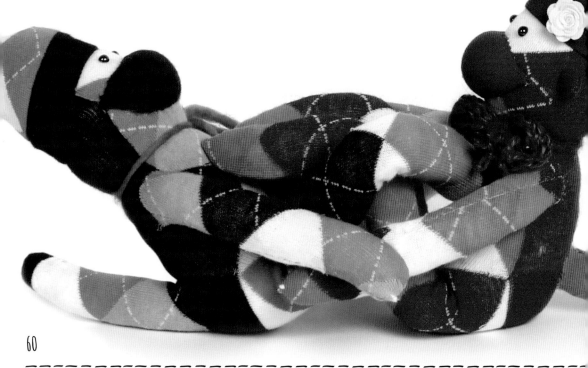

Seated face-to-face, the sock monkeys bring their feet to each other's chests and clasp hands while making love.

The lovers' limbs should intermingle as they darn and thread through their deepest desires. Balance is key, and sock monkeys should start slowly in their first attempts at this powerful position.

THE BUD

The girl sock monkey draws her limbs together, as tightly tucked as a sock rolled in on itself. With her arms holding her knees to her chest, her secret seam will be open as a beautiful flower, or a toe breaking through an old sock.

The boy monkey, crouched beside her, will find great delight in this pose. It allows him to rock his lover back and forth, so they both find the pleasure of a thousand unravelings.

FROM THE ANCIENT TEXT:

"When, with fabric feet set well-apart on the ground, the girl sock monkey folds, placing a paw upon each thigh, and the boy sock monkey takes her from the rear, it is called the Ass."

The boy sock monkey should caress and hold the girl sock monkey's waist so that she doesn't fall forward in this position. The girl sock monkey cannot use her arms for balance, so she must depend upon her partner's plush support to stay upright.

THE ASS

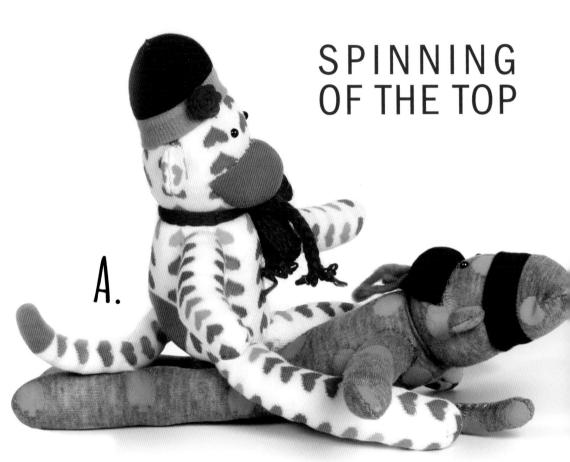

SPINNING
OF THE TOP

A.

B.

C.

FROM THE ANCIENT TEXT:

"While engaged in congress, the girl monkey sits upon her lover and turns round and round like a wheel, 'til both are satisfied and threadbare. This shall be called the Spinning of the Top."

This move requires a great deal of practice and care, lest the girl monkey turn too quickly and twist the boy monkey's secret seam, like laundry wrung out after a wash. Instead, the girl sock monkey should support herself by pushing her paws on the boy sock monkey's chest and thighs.

ONE KNOT

Sock monkeys should not be put off by the name of this position, which may bring to mind the troubles of tangled, loose threads. In fact, this is a simple position, best for the sock monkeys who want the enduring pleasure of *Sock Monkey Kama Sutra*, but fear their own ability to stretch without tearing.

FROM THE ANCIENT TEXT:
"The boy sock monkey kneels, taking his lover in his lap, and bending her forward until her argyle chest presses flush against her cotton-filled thighs."

THE REMEMBRANCE WHEEL

The boy sock monkey kneels on the ground, and takes his partner on his lap. Slowly, he stretches the girl sock monkey's legs out until they are perpendicular to the couple—like the foot to the leg.

Grasping his lover's feet with his paws, the boy sock monkey opens and closes her legs to give both sock animals pleasure.

THE MONKEY

FROM THE ANCIENT TEXT:

"The girl sock monkey sits upon the thighs of her kneeling lover, facing away from the bow around his neck. She grasps her own feet as the boy sock monkey places his paws on her waist and moves her to and fro."

By holding her close and undulating like a wave, or the curves between toes, the boy monkey is sure to hit all of his partner's most erotic threads. This is a tender position—and an excellent choice for sock monkeys who are easily snagged or torn.

WIDELY OPEN
POSITION

The girl sock monkey lowers her head until her hat rests on the ground, then uses her tail to raise the middle of her body. The result is that her spine curves like the instep of a foot. She must keep her legs far apart and her knit relaxed. This allows her thread to accommodate the boy sock monkey as he darns her secret seams.

For guaranteed enjoyment, the sock lovers may wish to use a lubricant, such as Tide or Downy. Fill the cap ¼ of the way up for short lovemaking sessions, ½ for mid-length delights, and ¾ for longer pleasures.

THE SWAN SPORT

This is a playful position, best for colorful socks monkeys who are full of adventure and secure in their stuffing.

The girl sock monkey rests upon her partner, facing away from his matching hat. She brings both of her feet up to his thighs, and works her hips with the rhythm of a washing machine on its last spin cycle.

MORE STUFFED PLEASURES
FOR INSATIABLE SOCK MONKEYS

Aside from the many positions of exotic intercourse and gratifying congress, *Sock Monkey Kama Sutra* also teaches readers how to use their mouths to bring each other to the height of pleasure. Through four kinds of kisses and the art of oral sex, sock monkeys throughout the world can bring each other divine, knitted happiness.

Practiced instead of sex, or as foreplay, these methods will ignite passion more quickly than a match to a linen fabric swatch.

THE STRAIGHT KISS

This is a simple kiss, made when the lips are in contact,
and both sock monkeys face each other straight on.

THE SLANTING KISS

This kiss requires one of the sock monkeys to slant their mouth diagonally against the other's lips.

THE TURNED KISS

In this kiss, one of the sock lovers turns up the face of
the other by holding the head and the chin.

THE PRESSED KISS

The pressed kiss takes place when any of the other three varieties is done with some force.

ORAL SEX
FOR THE BOY
SOCK MONKEY

Vatsyayana Banana had much to say on the subject of how a girl sock monkey could use her plush mouth to bring pleasure to a boy sock monkey's secret seam.

- **Touching:** "When the girl sock monkey takes the boy monkey's secret seam in hand and, shaping her lips to an 'O,' lays them lightly to its tip, moving her head in tiny circles, this is the first step."
- **Biting at the Sides:** "Next, grasping its head in her hand, she clamps her fabric mouth tightly about the shaft, first on one side then the other, taking great care that her teeth don't nick any threads."
- **Striking at the Tip:** "While kissing, she lets her tongue flick all over and then, pointing it, strikes repeatedly at the most sensitive stitching."
- **Swallowed Whole:** "When the girl monkey senses that the boy monkey will soon be overcome with pleasure, she swallows whole his secret seam, working upon it until he is as limp as a sock upon a clothesline."

ORAL SEX
FOR THE GIRL
SOCK MONKEY

Likewise, there is a method by which a lover can use its mouth to bring the girl sock monkey to new heights of pleasure.

- **Sucked Up:** "The boy sock monkey should cup and lift the girl monkey's firmly stuffed buttocks, letting his tongue-tip probe her navel, then sliding down to the secret seam."
- **The Quivering Kiss:** "With delicate paws, the boy sock monkey should pinch the fabric lips of her secret seam very, very slowly together, and kiss them as though he'd kissed her lower lip."
- **The Circling Tongue:** "Now he should let his tongue gently probe her secret seam, with his mouth slowly circling."
- **The Tongue Massage:** "He should let his tongue rest for a moment, poised on the first stitch of the girl sock monkey's secret seam, before beginning to vigorously stimulate his lover, as a toe wiggles to and fro."

FROM THE ANCIENT TEXT:

"If the pair of sock monkeys lie upon one another, facing opposite ways, and kiss each other's secret parts, it is known as the Crow."

Among contemporary society, this sock monkey position is best known as the "69." Sock partners must take care not to breathe in their lover's fiber through their nose, lest they choke on their pleasure.

THE CROW

MAKE YOUR OWN NAUGHTY SOCK MONKEYS

MATERIALS:

- One pair men's heavy-knit socks with contrasting heel and toe
- All-purpose sewing thread
- Polyester fiberfill or cotton batting for stuffing
- Black embroidery thread (if sewing on eyes)
- Two black buttons or stickers for eyes
- Knitting yarn that contrasts with the sock color

HEAD, BODY, AND LEGS:

1. Turn Sock 1 inside out. Sew a ½-inch seam (A) on both sides of the center of the sock, starting 3 inches from the heel and across the end of the sock cuff.
2. Cut sock between seams and to within 1½ inch of the heel.
3. Turn sock so seams are inside and stuff sock to make head, body, and legs.
4. Tie the knitting yarn in a bow below the sock monkey's head, creating the neck.

ARMS:

1. Cut the upper back (above the heel) portion of Sock 2 into two pieces.
2. Sew a ½-inch seam, right sides facing and rounding across the cuff end (B).
3. Turn right-side-out and stuff. Sew arms to body.

TAIL:

1. Cut a 1-inch strip from the front of Sock 2, ending at the toe and tapering to the cuff end.
2. Sew a ½-inch seam, right sides facing.
3. Turn right-side-out and stuff. Sew tail to body.

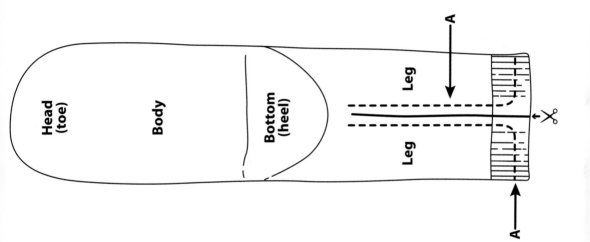

Head
(toe)

Body

Bottom
(heel)

Leg

Leg

A

A

✂

MOUTH:

1. Cut the heel from Sock 2, leaving an edge of contrasting color.
2. Attach to lower part of the face, sewing along the bottom. Stuff and finish sewing around the top.

CAP:

1. Cut off the toe of Sock 2, leaving ½ inch of contrasting color to roll for a brim.
2. Attach to the head. If desired, decorate with flowers or pompoms.

EARS:

1. Cut ears from the remaining sole of Sock 2. Sew a ½-inch seam around the outside of the ears, right sides facing.
2. Turn and stuff ears; sew to sides of head.

EYES:

1. Attach eyes to face, or sew on with embroidery thread.

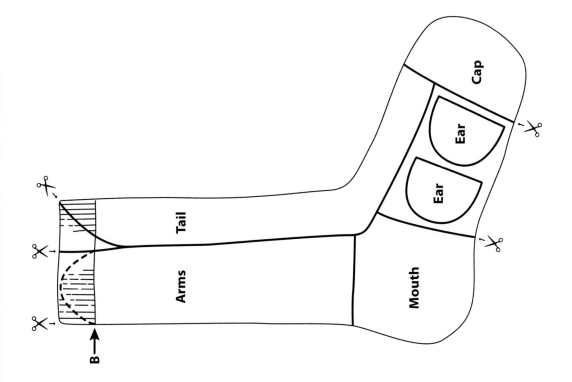

Cap

Ear

Ear

Tail

Arms

Mouth

B